Samplers & M...
IN CROSS STITCH.

Angela Davidson

MEREHURST

THE CHARTS

Some of the designs in this book are very detailed and, due to inevitable space limitations, the charts may be shown on a comparatively small scale; in such cases, readers may find it helpful to have the particular chart with which they are currently working enlarged.

THREADS

The projects in this book were all stitched with DMC stranded cotton embroidery threads. The keys given with each chart also list thread combinations for those who wish to use Anchor or Madeira embroidery threads. It should be pointed out that the shades produced by different companies vary slightly, and it is not always possible to find identical colours in a different range.

Published in 1998 by Merehurst Limited
Ferry House, 51-57 Lacy Road, Putney, London SW15 1PR
Copyright © 1998 Merehurst Limited
ISBN 1 85391 681 1

A catalogue record for this book is available from the British Library.

Edited by Diana Lodge
Designed by Maggie Aldred
Photography by Juliet Piddington
Illustrations by John Hutchinson and King & King
Colour separation by Bright Arts (H K) Ltd
Printed in Hong Kong by Wing King Tong

Merehurst is the leading publisher of craft books and has an excellent range of titles to suit all levels. Please send to the address above for our free catalogue, stating the title of this book.

CONTENTS

INTRODUCTION

Traditional samplers, of the type used to teach generations of children the art of embroidery, are still the most popular form of cross stitch design. In this book, I have tried to produce a collection of designs that includes traditional motifs and borders while giving some of the projects a more modern feel.

Feel free to alter any of the designs to suit yourself or the person for whom you are stitching it, or make up your own sampler using a selection of borders and motifs from different samplers. One of the delights of the format of the traditional sampler is that individual motifs and borders can so easily be copied and used elsewhere – on table linen, hand towels, small cards, mats, paperweights, keys rings and so on. Although most of the designs in this book have been stitched as samplers, perhaps with one or two additional suggestions, I hope that you will enjoy using elements from the samplers for your own purposes. Tiny motifs take so little time to stitch, and they can be used to give a personal touch to your gifts and household items.

Do not be afraid to experiment with different weights and colours of fabrics and use the wide selection of beads, charms and metallic threads now available. Remember that designs stitched on 28-count material (over two threads) will be of equal size to those stitched on 14-count material. Whether you decide to stitch the kitchen sampler or the smaller greetings card taken from the traditional sampler, I am hope you will gain as much enjoyment from your stitching as I did from designing each project.

BASIC SKILLS

BEFORE YOU BEGIN

PREPARING THE FABRIC
Even with an average amount of handling, many evenweave fabrics tend to fray at the edges, so it is a good idea to overcast the raw edges, using ordinary sewing thread, before you begin.

FABRIC
Most of the projects in this book use Aida fabric, which is ideal both for beginners and more advanced stitchers as it has a surface of clearly designated squares, each cross stitch being worked over a square. Other projects use evenweave Jobelan fabric, which has 28 threads per 2.5cm (1in) each way, but in these cases the stitches are worked over two threads.

All evenweaves have a count, referring to the number of Aida blocks, threads or perforations, per 2.5cm (1in) in each direction. The lower the count, therefore, the larger the finished stitching. If you wish to use fabric with a different stitch count, count the maximum number of stitches on the chart horizontally and vertically and divide these numbers by the stitch count of your chosen fabric; this will give you the dimensions of the design when stitched on your fabric.

THE INSTRUCTIONS
Each project begins with a full list of the materials that you will require. The measurements given for the embroidery fabric include a minimum of 5cm (2in) all around to allow for preparing the edges to prevent them from fraying.

Colour keys for stranded embroidery cottons — DMC, Anchor or Madeira — are given with each chart. It is assumed that you will need to buy one skein of each colour mentioned in a particular key, even though you may use less.

Where metallic threads have been used, the specific make of thread is listed, without giving any equivalent. Several manufacturers produce these threads, but each brand varies significantly, and it is not always possible to find a close equivalent. If you are unable to obtain the named thread, you may be able to substitute a similar thread for an equally attractive, if perhaps slightly different, effect, but you should experiment to ensure that you achieve a good coverage of the fabric before using it in your embroidery.

Before you begin to embroider, always mark the centre of the design with two lines of basting stitches, one vertical and one horizontal, running from edge to edge of the fabric, as indicated by the arrows on the charts.

As you stitch, use the centre lines given on the chart and the basting threads on your fabric as reference points for counting the squares and threads to position your design accurately.

SPACING MOTIFS

If you are taking motifs or elements from one design and making up a design of your own, it is important to make sure that the spacing is correct. To achieve this, subtract the number of stitches in the motif or alphabet from the total number of stitches in the design. Halve the difference and begin stitching at that point.

For example, if the width of your sampler is 69 stitches and the motif is 29 stitches wide, the difference will be 40 stitches, so allow 20 stitches in from the edge of sampler and begin stitching the motif (20 stitches, motif, 20 stitches). If you are working a band sampler, leave an equal number of free lines between bands for a better overall effect.

BORDERS

The easiest way to make your chosen border turn a corner is to chart your design on graph paper, using each square of the paper as one cross stitch. Take a small handbag mirror and position it diagonally across the design. You will then be able to chart the reverse image as seen in the mirror.

WORKING IN A HOOP

A hoop is the most popular frame for use with small areas of embroidery. It consists of two rings, one fitted inside the other; the outer ring usually has an adjustable screw attachment so that it can be tightened to hold the stretched fabric in place. To avoid marking the fabric, remove the embroidery from the hoop between stitching sessions. Hoops are available in several sizes, ranging from 10cm (4in) in diameter to quilting hoops with a diameter of 38cm (15in). Hoops with table stands or floor stands attached are also available.

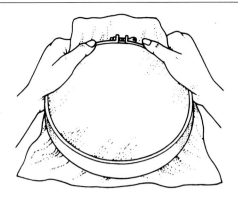

1 To stretch your fabric in a hoop, place the area to be embroidered over the inner ring and press the outer ring over it, with the tension screw released. Tissue paper can be placed between the outer ring and the embroidery, so that the hoop does not mark the fabric. Lay the tissue paper over the fabric when you set it in the hoop, then tear away the central embroidery area.

2 Smooth the fabric and, if necessary, straighten the grain before tightening the screw. The fabric should be evenly stretched.

WORKING IN A RECTANGULAR FRAME

Rectangular frames are more suitable for larger pieces of embroidery. They consist of two rollers, with tapes attached, and two flat side pieces, which slot into the rollers and are held in place by pegs or screw attachments. Available in different sizes, either alone or with adjustable table or floor stands, frames are measured by the length of the roller tape, and range in size from 30cm (12in) to 68cm (27in).

As alternatives to a slate frame, canvas stretchers and the backs of old picture frames can be used. Provided there is sufficient extra fabric around the finished size of the embroidery, the edges can be turned under and simply attached with drawing pins (thumb tacks) or staples.

1 To stretch your fabric in a rectangular frame, cut out the fabric, allowing at least an extra 5cm (2in)

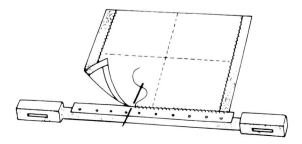

all around the finished size of the embroidery. Baste a single 12mm (1/2in) turning on the top and bottom edges and oversew strong tape, 2.5cm (1in) wide, to the other two sides. Mark the centre line both ways with basting stitches. Working from the centre outward and using strong thread, oversew the top and bottom edges to the roller tapes. Fit the side pieces into the slots and roll any extra fabric on one roller until the fabric is taut.

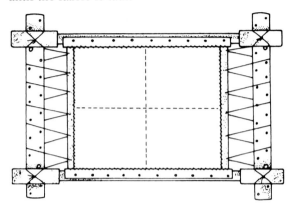

2 Insert the pegs or adjust the screw attachments to secure the frame. Thread a large-eyed needle (chenille needle) with strong thread or fine string and lace both edges, securing the ends around the intersections of the frame. Lace the webbing at 2.5cm (1in) intervals, stretching the fabric evenly.

EXTENDING EMBROIDERY FABRIC

It is easy to extend a piece of embroidery fabric, such as a bookmark, to stretch it in a hoop.
• Fabric oddments of a similar weight can be used. Simply cut four pieces to size (in other words, to the measurement that will fit both the embroidery fabric and your hoop) and baste them to each side of the embroidery fabric before stretching it in the hoop in the usual way.

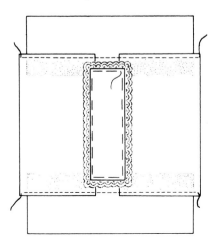

CROSS STITCH

For all cross stitch embroidery, the following two methods of working are used. In each case, neat rows of vertical stitches are produced on the back of the fabric.

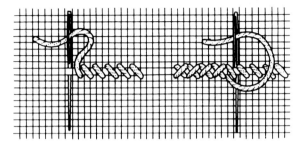

• When stitching large areas, work in horizontal rows. Working from right to left, complete the first row of evenly spaced diagonal stitches over the number of threads specified in the project instructions. Then, working from left to right, repeat the process. Continue in this way, making sure each stitch crosses in the same direction.

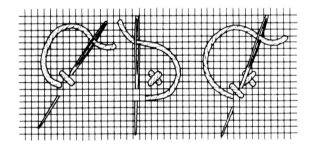

• When stitching diagonal lines, work downwards, completing each stitch before moving to the next. When starting a project, always begin to embroider at the centre of the design and work outwards to ensure that the design will be placed centrally on the fabric.

BACKSTITCH

Backstitch is used in the projects to give emphasis to a particular foldline, an outline or a shadow. The stitches are worked over the same number of threads as the cross stitches, forming continuous straight or diagonal lines.

• Make the first stitch from left to right; pass the needle behind the fabric and bring it out one stitch length ahead to the left. Repeat and continue in this way along the line.

To give a rounded effect on curves in some designs, backstitch is laid over two squares to give a 'long-line' and is usually placed over a three-quarter stitch which fills the largest portion of the fabric to be outlined.

THREE-QUARTER CROSS STITCH

Some fractional stitches are used on certain projects in this book; although they strike fear into the hearts of less experienced stitchers they are not difficult to master, and give a more natural line in certain instances. Should you find it difficult to pierce the centre of the Aida block, simply use a sharp needle to make a small hole in the centre first.

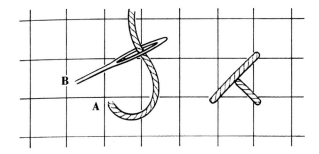

To work a three-quarter cross stitch, bring the needle up at point A and down through the centre of the square at B. Later, a diagonal backstitch finishes the stitch. A chart square with two different symbols separated by a diagonal line requires two 'three-quarter' stitches. Backstitch will later finish the square.

THREADING TECHNIQUES FOR METALLIC THREADS AND BLENDING FILAMENTS

You should use no more than 45cm (18in) of thread at a time. Double the thread about 5cm (2in) at one end, and inset the loop through the eye of the needle. Pull the loop over the point of the needle and gently pull the loop towards the end of the eye to secure the thread to the needle. If you are using a combination of blending filament and stranded cotton, thread the latter through the eye in the usual way, and clip it to match the length of the blending filament.

FINISHING

MOUNTING EMBROIDERY

The cardboard should be cut to the size of the finished embroidery, with an extra amount added all round to allow for the recess in the frame.

LIGHTWEIGHT FABRICS

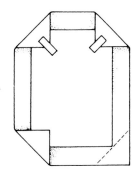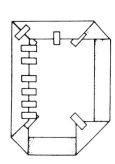

1 Place the embroidery face down, with the cardboard centred on top, and basting and pencil lines matching. Begin by folding over the fabric at each corner and securing it with masking tape.

2 Working first on one side and then the other, fold over the fabric on all sides and secure it firmly with pieces of masking tape, placed about 2.5cm (1in) apart. Also neaten the mitred corners with masking tape, pulling the fabric tightly to give a firm, smooth finish.

HEAVIER FABRICS

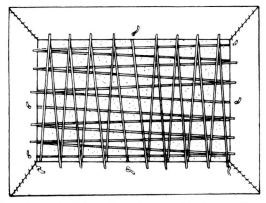

Lay the embroidery face down, with the cardboard centred on top; fold over the edges of the fabric on opposite sides, making mitred folds at the corners, and lace across, using strong thread. Repeat on the other two sides. Finally, pull up the fabric firmly over the cardboard. Overstitch the mitred corners.

Traditional Sampler

Several traditional motifs – the vine, acorn and carnation, the latter representing maternal love – are combined in this sampler and greetings card. The muted colours have been chosen to give a feeling of age.

TRADITIONAL SAMPLER

YOU WILL NEED

For the sampler, set in a frame with an external measurement of 34.5cm x 42cm (13½in x 16½in), and a double mount with an aperture measuring 20.5cm x 28.5cm (8¼in x 11¼in):

33cm x 39.5cm (13in x 15½in) of 28-count Jobelan fabric, in bone
Stranded embroidery cotton in the colours given in the appropriate panel
No 26 tapestry needle
Frame and mounts of your choice
Strong thread for lacing across the back when mounting
Stiff cardboard, cut to fit inside the frame recess, for mounting

Note: to add to the effect, two mounts have been used – a dark blue mount, with an aperture as specified above, and a maroon mount, with an aperture 1cm (½in) larger each way, to reveal the blue mount.

For the card, with an aperture 8cm (3¼in) square:

13cm (5in) square of 28-count Jobelan fabric, in ivory
Stranded embroidery cotton in the colours given in the appropriate panel
No 26 tapestry needle
Card (for suppliers, see page 40)

●

THE EMBROIDERY

To embroider the sampler, first prepare the fabric (see page 4), marking the centre both ways with horizontal and vertical lines of basting stitches. Set the fabric in a hoop or frame (see page 5) and start your embroidery from the centre of the design, completing all cross stitches first and using two strands of embroidery cotton in the needle. Make sure each cross stitch covers two threads of fabric. Finish with the backstitches, this time using one strand of embroidery cotton. When stitching is complete, hand wash the embroidery if necessary and press gently on the wrong side with a steam iron.

If you are making the card, prepare your fabric as above and commence stitching from the centre of

the chart. Complete all cross stitches, using two strands of thread in the needle. If necessary, hand wash the finished embroidery and press gently on the wrong side.

ASSEMBLY

Using the basting stitches as guidelines, centre the sampler over the cardboard mount. Lace the embroidery over the mount, following the instructions on page 7. When you have finished, gently remove the basting stitches. Place the two mounts and then the mounted embroidery into the frame, and complete assembly, according to the manufacturer's instructions.

For the card, keeping the embroidery centred, trim the fabric to fit the card aperture and complete the assembly, following the manufacturer's instructions. You may find that you need to use either a small amount of all-purpose glue or double-sided tape to seal the card.

▼ CARD		DMC	ANCHOR	MADEIRA
–	Dark gold	680	901	2210
8	Blue	930	922	1712
■	Light gold	3046	887	2206

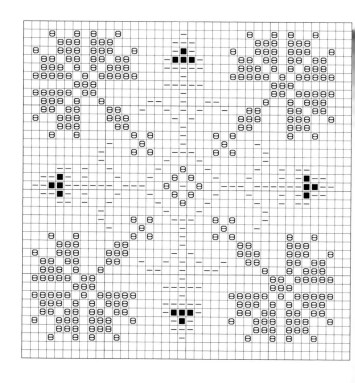

abcdefghijklmnop qrstuvwxyz

▲ **TRADITIONAL SAMPLER**

		DMC	ANCHOR	MADEIRA			DMC	ANCHOR	MADEIRA
1	Dark grey green	520	862	1505	N	Light brown	840	898	1912
2	Light grey green	522	860	1513	/	Very light brown	842	831	1910
−	Dark gold	680	901	2210	8	Blue	930	922	1712
3	Dark red	814	45	0514	H	Very dark green	934	862	1506
X	Brown	838	380	1914	■	Light gold	3046	887	2206

Note: backstitch vine leaves in light grey green, grapes in dark red, lower case alphabet in same colour sequence as large alphabet, and flower tendrils in the flower colour.

Kitchen Herbs

Topiary trees and fresh green herbs bring a breath of spring to this design for the kitchen. The design is accompanied by a matching hand towel for a ray of sunshine that will be with you every day.

KITCHEN HERBS

YOU WILL NEED

For the sampler, set in frame measuring 28.5cm x 29.5cm (11in x 11½in) externally, and with an aperture 18.5cm (7½in) square:

33cm (13in) square of 14-count Aida fabric, in mint green
Stranded embroidery cotton in the colours given in the appropriate panel
No 26 tapestry needle
Frame and mount of your choice, with an aperture as specified above
Strong thread for lacing across the back when mounting
Stiff cardboard, cut to fit inside the frame recess, for mounting

For the hand towel, measuring 48cm x 26cm (19in x 10½in) approximately, including fringe, with an Aida band (2½in) deep:

Stranded embroidery cotton in the colours given in the appropriate panel
No 26 tapestry needle
Hand towel (for suppliers, see page 40)

Note: if you wish to embroider this design on a towel that does not have an Aida band already attached to it, you can stitch Aida band to any towel of your choice; allow for a 12mm (½in) turning at each end and count the number of Aida blocks across the width of the band (less turnings) so that you can space pattern repeats evenly, working from the centre out to the side edges of the towel.

●

THE EMBROIDERY

For the framed picture, first prepare the fabric, marking the centre with vertical and horizontal lines of basting stitches. Set the fabric in a hoop or frame (see page 5) and complete the embroidery, using two strands of embroidery cotton throughout the design. If necessary, hand wash and gently press the finished embroidery on the wrong side.

If you are embroidering the hand towel, it is most important to ensure that you repeat the design evenly across the towel and leave an equal amount of material above and below the design. Find the centre of the Aida band by folding it in half; baste down the centre and across the centre, from side to side of the towel. Centre the design on the Aida band and start stitching, working outwards to each side. Use two strands of embroidery cotton throughout the design. When the embroidery is completed, remove basting stitches.

MOUNTING THE PICTURE

Mark the cardboard with horizontal and vertical centre lines and make sure the embroidery is centered over the cardboard mount by aligning it with the basting stitches. Lace the embroidery over the mount (see page 7); remove basting stitches, and complete the assembly, following the manufacturer's instructions.

▶ **KITCHEN SAMPLER**

		DMC	ANCHOR	MADEIRA
■	Bright white	B5200	1	White
I	Very dark green	699	923	1303
2	Dark green	700	228	1304
3	Medium green	702	226	1306
0	Light green	704	256	1411
/	Light terracotta	3776	1048	0402
∃	Dark terracotta	3777	1015	0401

▶ **TOWEL**

		DMC	ANCHOR	MADEIRA
3	Medium green	702	226	1306
◀	Light green	704	256	1411
/	Light terracotta	3776	1048	0402
2	Dark terracotta	3777	1015	0401
−	Yellow	743	302	913

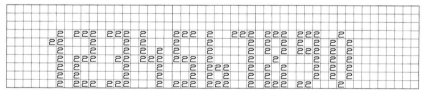

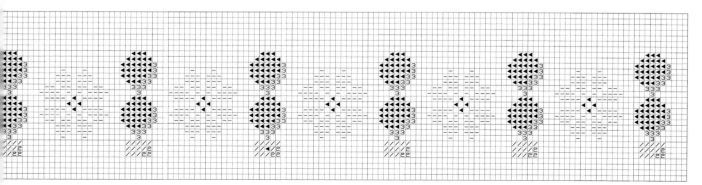

For a New Arrival

Welcome the arrival of a new baby with this sampler in beautiful pastel shades. Rocking horses in brighter, bolder colours look lovely on the baby's bib, and the sampler motifs could also be repeated on covers or clothing.

FOR A NEW ARRIVAL

YOU WILL NEED

For the sampler, set in frame with an external measurement of 26cm x 22cm (10½in x 8¾in) and an aperture measuring 23cm x 19cm (9in x 7½in):

33cm x 35.5cm (13in x 14in) of 28-count Jobelan fabric, in pale lemon
Stranded embroidery cotton in the colours given in the appropriate panel
No 26 tapestry needle
Frame of your choice
Strong thread, for lacing across the back when mounting
Stiff cardboard, cut to fit inside the frame recess, for mounting

For the baby's bib, measuring 28cm (11in) across and 33cm (13in) deep at the front:

Stranded embroidery cotton in the colours given in the appropriate panel
No 26 tapestry needle
Baby's bib with Aida insert (for suppliers, see page 40)

•

THE EMBROIDERY

For the sampler, first prepare the fabric, marking horizontal and vertical centre lines with basting stitches. Set the fabric in a hoop or frame (see page 5) and then, following the chart, complete all cross stitches first, using two strands of embroidery cotton. Make sure that each cross stitch covers two threads of fabric. Finish with the backstitching, using one strand of embroidery cotton.

For the baby's bib, find the centre of the Aida insert at the front by folding the bib in half; baste down the centre and across the fabric on the centre line. Holding the bib in your hand, begin stitching from the centre of the design, working outwards.

Check that you have the same number of squares above and below the design.

MOUNTING THE PICTURE

Mark the cardboard with horizontal and vertical centre lines and make sure the embroidery is centered over the cardboard mount by aligning it with the basting stitches. Lace the embroidery over the mount (see page 7); remove basting stitches, and complete the assembly, following the manufacturer's instructions.

▶ NEW ARRIVAL SAMPLER			
	DMC	ANCHOR	MADEIRA
– Lilac	211	342	0801
2 Yellow	727	293	0110
I Pink	3689	49	0607
И Green	369	1043	1309
X Turquoise	964	185	1112
S Dark green	913	204	1212
T Dark blue	322	978	1004
8 Blue	3325	129	1002
■ White	B2500	1	White
Dark turquoise*	958	187	1202

Note: backstitch the baby's name and date of birth in dark turquoise* (used for backstitching only) and the balloon strings in same colour as the teddy holding the balloon.

▼ BABY'S BIB			
	DMC	ANCHOR	MADEIRA
– Yellow	727	293	0110
2 Dark green	991	189	1204
3 Pale green	993	186	1201
▼ Dark apricot	3340	329	0214
O Pale apricot	3341	328	0301

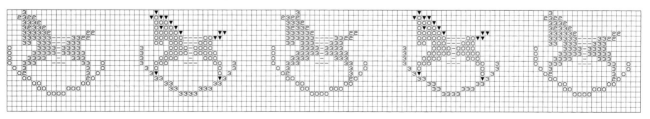

20 February 1998
Thomas James

ABCDEFGHIJKLMNOPQRSTUVWXYZ

abcdefghijklmnopqrstuvwxyz

1234567890

ABCDEF
GHIJKL
MNOPQ
The Moon and Stars
Will take care of you
RSTUV
WXYZ

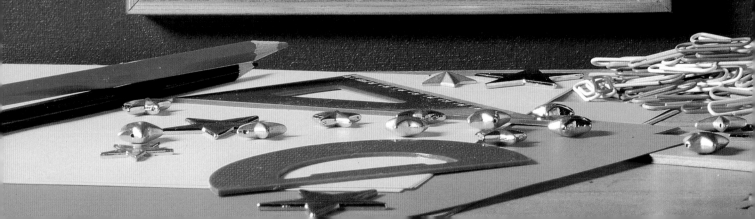

Moon and Stars

The moon and stars sampler, with its pretty metallic threads and tiny charms, would make a delightful gift for a daughter or friend. The pen and pencil holder could equally well be used to hold ear-rings or small change.

MOON AND STARS

YOU WILL NEED

For sampler, set in frame with an external measurement of 20.5cm x 26.5cm (8in x 10½in):

28cm x 35cm (11in x 13¾in) of 28-count Jobelan fabric, in navy
Stranded embroidery cotton in colours given in the appropriate panel
Kreinik gold metallic thread
Moon and stars charms (for suppliers, see page 40)
No 26 tapestry needle
Frame of your choice
Strong thread, for lacing across the back when mounting
Stiff cardboard, cut to fit inside the frame recess, for mounting

Note: Kreinik gold metallic thread has been used; there is no exact equivalent for this in either of the other brands listed, but you can substitute a different thread, provided you obtain an attractive effect.

For the triangular pen or pencil holder, 10cm (4in) high, with sides 9cm (3½in) across:

Three 15cm (6in) squares of 14-count Aida fabric, in navy blue
Stranded embroidery cotton in the colours given in the appropriate panel
No 26 tapestry needle
Three 9cm x 8cm (3½in x 3⅛in) pieces of thin navy card, for backing
Pen/pencil holder (for suppliers, see page 40)

Note: all three sides of the pencil holder are the same, so you may prefer to stitch the repeats on a single piece of fabric and cut it up later, in which case you will require 15cm x 32cm (6in x 12½in) of fabric

●

THE EMBROIDERY

For the sampler, first prepare the fabric (see page 4), marking the centre with horizontal and vertical lines of basting stitches. Set the fabric in a hoop or frame (see page 5) and then, following the chart, start from the centre of the design and work outwards. Embroider all the cross stitches first, using two strands of embroidery cotton. Make sure each cross

stitch covers two threads of the fabric. This design contains three-quarter stitches (see page 6); these are marked on the chart with very small symbols. Back stitch, using one strand of the metallic thread, and attach the charms when all stitching is completed.

For the pencil holder, prepare the fabric for each side (see page 4), marking the centre with horizontal and vertical lines of basting stitches. If you are using a single piece of fabric, baste a rectangle with lines 2.5cm (1in) from the edge on each side, then divide the rectangle into three equal rectangles, each 10cm x 9cm (4in x 3½in). Mark the centre of each rectangle vertically and horizontally in the usual way.

▼ **PEN AND PENCIL HOLDER**

		DMC	ANCHOR	MADEIRA
2	Bottle green	890	683	1314
3	Yellow	743	302	0113
L	Grey	647	1040	1813
–	Orange	742	303	0114
K	Black	310	403	Black
8	Dull green	935	861	1514

Note: backstitch the star rays in yellow.

The design is repeated on all sides. For each design, find the centre point of the chart and begin stitching from the marked centre of your fabric. Complete all cross stitches first. Both cross stitch and backstitch details should be completed using two strands of embroidery cotton.

ASSEMBLY

For the sampler, mark the central horizontal and vertical lines on the cardboard and align these with the lines of basting stitches. Lace the embroidery over the mount, following the instructions on page 7. Remove the basting stitches and set picture in your chosen frame.

For the pencil holder, keeping the design centred, trim each square of fabric, or cut the stitched repeats apart, to measure the three pieces of navy card. For each side, glue a piece of card to the back of the material and insert in the aperture, following the manufacturer's instructions.

▲ MOON AND STARS SAMPLER

		DMC	ANCHOR	MADEIRA
3	Yellow	743	302	0113
−	Orange	742	303	0114
	Gold	Kreinik metallic gold thread, very fine (4) braid 202HL		

Note: backstitch the lettering in orange, using one strand of embroidery cotton, and stitch the star rays with metallic thread.

Merry Christmas!

The combination of traditional Christmas colours and small gold beads gives a festive sparkle to this band sampler. Use the individual motifs to make attractive greetings cards for friends and family.

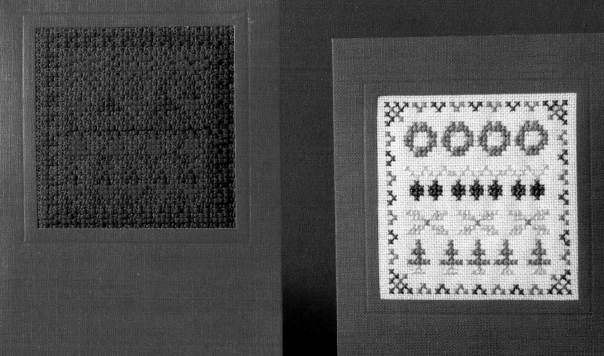

MERRY CHRISTMAS!

YOU WILL NEED

For the sampler, set in a frame with an external measurement of 20.5cm x 28cm (8in x 11in) and an aperture measuring 16.5cm x 24cm (6¹/₂in x 9¹/₂in):

30.5 x 38cm (12in x15in) of 28-count Jobelan fabric, in silver lurex
No 26 tapestry needle
Stranded embroidery cotton in the colours given in the appropriate panel
Mill Hill gold beads No 00557
White cotton and beading needle, for attaching the beads
Frame as specified above
Strong thread, for lacing across the back when mounting
Stiff cardboard, cut to fit inside the frame recess, for mounting

For the red greetings card, with an aperture measuring 7.5cm (3in) square:

13cm (5in) square of 14-count Aida fabric, in Christmas green
Stranded embroidery cotton in the colours given in the appropriate panel
No 26 tapestry needle
Greetings card (for suppliers, see page 40)

For the green card, with an aperture measuring 7.5cm (3in) square:

13cm (5in) square of 28-count Jobelan fabric, in antique white
Stranded embroidery cotton in the colours given in the appropriate panel
Kreinik silver metallic thread
No 26 tapestry needle
Greetings card (for suppliers, see page 40)

●

THE EMBROIDERY

For the framed picture, first prepare the fabric (see page 4), marking the centre with horizontal and vertical lines of basting stitches. Set the fabric in a hoop or frame (see page 5) and then, following the chart, start from the centre of the design and work outwards. Use two strands of embroidery cotton for the cross stitches, making sure each cross stitch

▼ RED CARD	DMC	ANCHOR	MADEIRA
I Bright Christmas red	321	9046	0510
3 Dark Christmas red	814	45	0514

▼ GREEN CARD	DMC	ANCHOR	MADEIRA
● Dark green	895	1044	1405
Y Light green	3363	262	1602
V Silver	Kreinik metallic thread, very fine (4) braid 001		

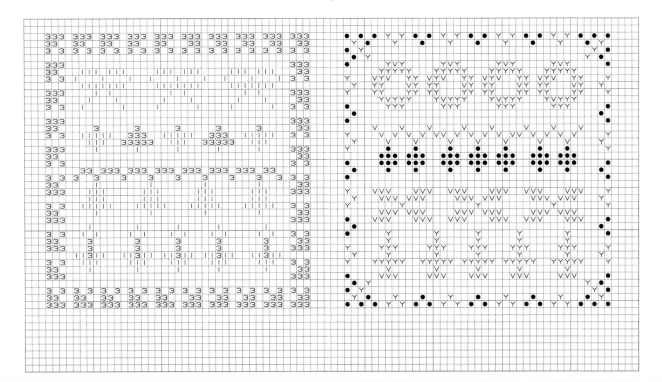

covers two threads of the fabric. Complete all the design before attaching the gold beads, using half cross stitch. Hand wash the finished embroidery if necessary and press carefully on the wrong side.

For each card, find the centre of your material and begin stitching from the centre of the chart, using two strands of thread in the needle when stitching with embroidery cotton or one strand when using the metallic thread. If you are stitching the green card, which is on Jobelan fabric, make sure each cross stitch covers two fabric threads.

ASSEMBLY

Using the basting stitches as guidelines, centre the finished embroidery over the cardboard mount, which should have been cut to fit the chosen frame. Lace the embroidery over the mount following the instructions on page 7. When you have finished, gently remove the basting stitches. Place the mounted embroidery into the frame, and complete the assembly, according to the manufacturer's instructions.

For each card, keeping the embroidery centred, trim the fabric to fit the card aperture and complete the assembly, following the manufacturer's instructions. You may find that you need to use a small amount of all-purpose glue or double-sided tape to seal the card.

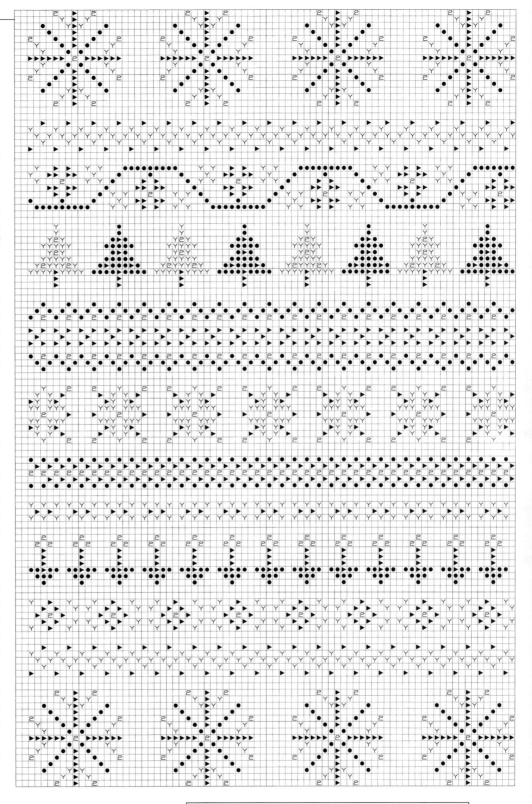

▲ CHRISTMAS SAMPLER			
	DMC	ANCHOR	MADEIRA
▶ Christmas red	815	43	0513
• Dark green	895	1044	1405
Y Light green	3363	262	1602
2 Gold bead			

A Modern Sampler

Stunning colours and a bright frame have been used to create a completely different sampler. It is accompanied by a trinket box in colours you might not normally think of combining, but the effect is striking.

A MODERN SAMPLER

YOU WILL NEED

For the sampler, set in a frame with an external measurement 27cm (10¼in) square and an aperture 23cm (9in) square:

40cm (16in) square of 28-count Jobelan fabric, in white
Stranded embroidery cotton in the colours given in the appropriate panel
No 26 tapestry needle
Frame of your choice
Strong thread, for lacing across the back when mounting
Stiff cardboard, cut to fit inside the frame recess, for mounting

For the trinket box, with aperture 9cm (3½in) in diameter:

13cm (5in) square of 14-count Aida fabric, in Christmas red
Stranded embroidery cotton in the colours given in the appropriate panel
No 26 tapestry needle
Red enamelled trinket box (for suppliers, see page 40)

•

THE EMBROIDERY

For the framed picture, first prepare the fabric (see page 4), marking the centre with horizontal and vertical lines of basting stitches. Set the fabric in a hoop or frame (see page 5) and then, following the chart, start from the centre of the design and work outwards. Use two strands of embroidery cotton for the cross stitches, making sure each cross stitch covers two threads of the fabric. Hand wash the finished embroidery, if necessary, and press gently on the wrong side with a steam iron.

For the enamelled box, prepare the fabric (see page 4) and find the centre point. Commence stitching from the centre of the design, using two strands of embroidery cotton throughout. Hand wash the finished embroidery, if necessary, and press gently on the wrong side with a steam iron.

ASSEMBLY

Using the basting stitches as guidelines, centre the finished embroidery over the cardboard mount, which should have been cut to fit the chosen frame. Lace the embroidery over the mount, following the instructions on page 7. When you have finished, gently remove the basting stitches. Place the mounted embroidery in the frame, and complete assembly, according to the manufacturer's instructions.

For the enamelled box, use the template provided with the box to trim the fabric to fit the lid aperture (you may find it easier to keep the design centred if you leave the basting stitches in position until the fabric has been trimmed to shape). Complete assembly, following the manufacturer's instructions.

▼ BOX		DMC	ANCHOR	MADEIRA
☑	Bright orange	608	332	0207
▶	Lemon	743	302	0113
Y	Medium orange	741	304	0201

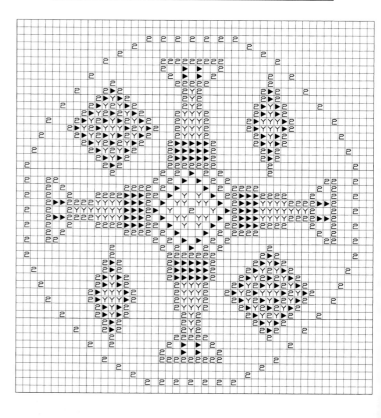

▲ MODERN SAMPLER				
		DMC	ANCHOR	MADEIRA
2	Bright orange	608	332	0207
■	Bright blue	995	410	1102
→	Sea green	943	188	1203
∧	Pink	718	88	0707
8	Dark blue	820	134	0914

United in Marriage

This band sampler is simple but very effective. You may like to alter the colours to match the bridesmaids' dresses or the wedding bouquets. The powder compact could be a gift from the bride to a bridesmaid.

UNITED IN MARRIAGE

YOU WILL NEED

For the sampler, set in frame with an external measurement of 26cm x 41.5cm (10¼in x 16in) and a double mount with an aperture measuring 14cm x 29cm (5¾in x 11⅜in):

28cm x 41.5cm (11in x 16½in) of 28-count Annabelle fabric, in blue/grey
Stranded embroidery cotton in the colours given in the appropriate panel
No 26 tapestry needle
Mount(s) with an aperture as specified above
Frame of your choice
Strong thread, for lacing across the back when mounting
Stiff cardboard, cut to fit inside the frame recess, for mounting

Note: to add to the effect, two mounts have been used – a cream mount, with an aperture as specified above, and a blue mount, with an aperture 1cm (½in) larger each way, to reveal the cream mount.

For the powder compact with an inset measuring 6.5cm (2¼in) in diameter

12.5cm (5in) square of 28-count Jobelan fabric, in antique white
Stranded embroidery cotton in the colours given in the appropriate panel
No 26 tapestry needle
Powder compact (for suppliers, see page 40)

●

THE EMBROIDERY

For the sampler, first prepare the fabric (see page 4), marking the centre with horizontal and vertical lines of basting stitches. Set the fabric in a hoop or frame (see page 5) and then, following the chart, start from the centre of the design and work outwards. Use two strands of embroidery cotton for the cross stitches, making sure each cross stitch covers two threads of the fabric. Finish with the backstitching, again using two strands of embroidery cotton.

For the powder compact, prepare the fabric (see page 4). Beginning from the centre of the chart, embroider the motif, using two strands of embroi-

dery cotton and making sure each cross stitch covers two threads of fabric.

Hand wash the finished embroideries, if necessary, and press gently on the wrong side with a steam iron.

ASSEMBLY

Using the basting stitches as guidelines, centre the sampler over the cardboard mount, which should have been cut to fit the chosen frame. Lace the embroidery over the mount, following the instructions on page 7. When you have finished, gently remove the basting stitches. Place the two mounts and then the mounted embroidery into the frame, and complete assembly, according to the manufacturer's instructions.

For the powder compact, use the template provided with the compact to trim the fabric to fit the lid inset (you may find it easier to keep the design centred if you leave the basting stitches in position until the fabric has been trimmed to shape). Complete assembly, following the manufacturer's instructions.

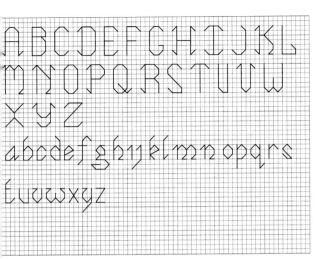

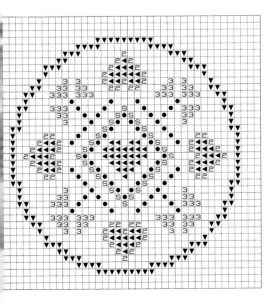

New Home Key Cupboard

Welcome friends or family to their new home with this delightful key box sampler. Complete your gift and stitch a key ring design of your choice.

NEW HOME KEY CUPBOARD

YOU WILL NEED

For the key cupboard, with an aperture measuring 17.5cm x 22.5cm (7in x 8¾in):

30cm x 35cm (12in x 14in) of 28-count Jobelan fabric, in white
Stranded embroidery cotton in the colours given in the appropriate panel
No 26 tapestry needle
Strong thread, for lacing across the back when mounting
Stiff cardboard, cut to fit inside the frame recess, for mounting
White distressed key cupboard (for suppliers, see page 40)

For the key rings, with embroidered insets approximately 3.2cm (1¼in) square or the same in diameter:

Remnants of 28-count of Jobelan fabric, in antique white
Stranded embroidery cotton in the colours given in the appropriate panel
No 26 tapestry needle
Round and square key rings (for suppliers, see page 40)

•

THE EMBROIDERY

For the key cupboard design, first prepare the fabric (see page 4), marking the centre with horizontal and vertical lines of basting stitches. Set the fabric in a hoop or frame (see page 5) and then, following the chart, start from the centre of the design and work outwards. Use two strands of embroidery cotton for the cross stitches, making sure each cross stitch covers two threads of the fabric. Finish with the backstitching, again using two strands of embroidery cotton. Hand wash the finished embroidery, if necessary, and press gently on the wrong side with a steam iron.

The tiny key ring designs can easily be stitched on scraps or a single piece of fabric. Use two strands of embroidery cotton for the cross stitches; each cross stitch should cover two crossed threads of the

Jobelan fabric. Make sure that you leave enough space around each design for cutting out.

ASSEMBLY

For the key cupboard, mark horizontal and vertical lines on the cardboard mount and align these with the basting stitches on the embroidery. Lace the embroidery over the mount, following the instructions on page 7. When you have finished, gently remove the basting stitches. Place the mounted embroidery in the door frame, and complete the assembly, according to the manufacturer's instructions.

For each key ring, keeping the design centred, trim the fabric to fit the aperture and complete the assembly, following the manufacturer's instructions.

▼ KEY RINGS		DMC	ANCHOR	MADEIRA
▼	Light blue	3325	129	1002
H	Pink	3326	36	0504
::	Brown	434	310	2009
O	Grass green	367	217	1312
I	Dark blue	334	977	1003

Note: if you are only making one key ring, you will not require all the colours listed.

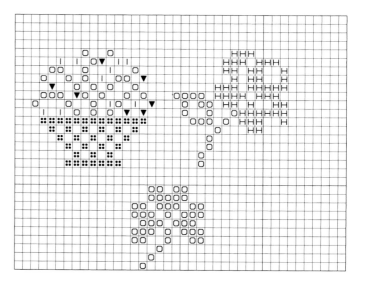

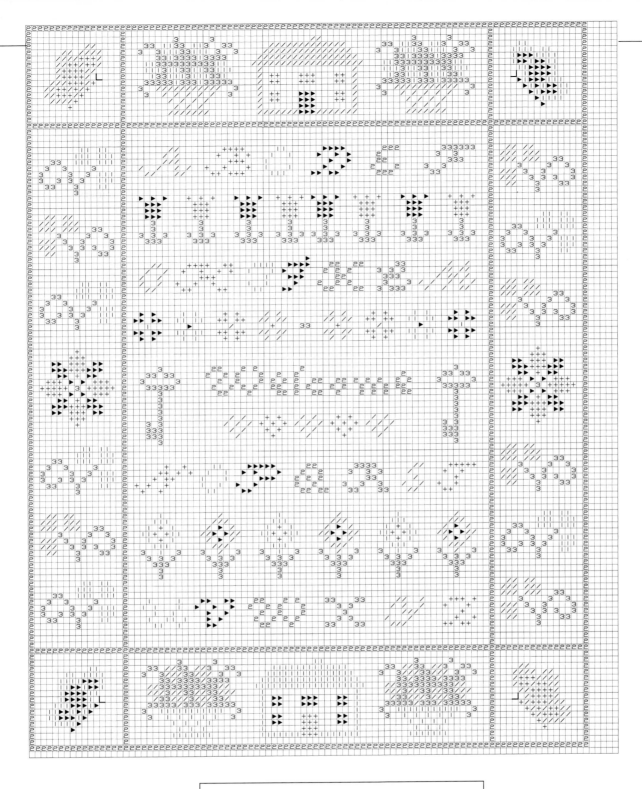

▲ KEY CUPBOARD			
	DMC	ANCHOR	MADEIRA
▶ Light blue	3325	129	1002
	Dark blue	334	977	1003
2 Yellow/green	3347	266	1501
3 Light yellow/green	3348	264	1409
+ Pale apricot	353	6	0304
/ Dark apricot	352	9	0303

Note: backstitch butterfly feelers in butterfly colour.

ACKNOWLEDGEMENTS

I would like to thank all my family for their support, in particular my husband for letting me take over his computer, my mother for introducing me to cross stitch, and my twin daughters and my son who suggested I should write a book. My grateful thanks also to Paula and Brian from The Studio Framing Shop, Poole, Dorset, for their expertise in selecting all the mounts and frames for the samplers; Janet, Jill, Jan and Jean, formerly of Wessex Needlecraft, Poole, for their advice and encouragement over the past years. Last but not least, my thanks to Jane Greenoff, who also encouraged me to design and produce a book.

SUPPLIERS

The cards on pages 8 and 24 were supplied by Craft Creations. Some of the fabrics were supplied by Fabric Flair Limited. The towel on page 12 was supplied by Crafters' Pride. The key cupboard (page 36) was supplied by S & A Frames.

The bib (page 16), pen/pencil holder (page 20), trinket box (page 28), powder compact (page 32) and key rings (page 36) were supplied by Framecraft Miniatures Limited, a mail order company that is a useful source of supply for many cross stitch items, including blank embroidery cards, picture frames and linens.

Craft Creations
Ingersoll House
Delamare Road
Cheshunt
Hertfordshire EN8 9ND
Telephone 01992 781900

Crafters' Pride
Macleod Craft Marketing
West Yonderton
Warlock Road
Bridge of Weir
Renfrewshire PA11 3SR
Telephone: 01505 612618

Fabric Flair Limited
Unit 3
Northland Industrial Estate
Copheap Lane
Warminster,
Wiltshire, BA12 0BG
Telephone: 01985 846 400

S & A Frames
The Old Post Office
Yarra Road
Cleethorpes
North Lincolnshire
DN35 8LS
Telephone: 01472 697772

FRAMECRAFT
Framecraft Miniatures Ltd
372-376 Summer Lane
Hockley
Birmingham
B19 3QA
Telephone: 0121 212 0551

Addresses for Framecraft stockists worldwide
Ireland Needlecraft Pty Ltd
2-4 Keppel Drive
Hallam, Victoria 3803
Australia

Danish Art Needlework
P.O. Box 442, Lethbridge
Alberta T1J 3Z1
Canada

Sanyei Imports
P.O. Box 5, Hashima Shi
Gifu 501-62, Japan

The Embroidery Shop
286 Queen Street
Masterton, New Zealand

Anne Brinkley Designs Inc.
246 Walnut Street
Newton, Mass. 02160
USA

S A Threads and Cottons Ltd
43 Somerset Road
Cape Town, South Africa

For more information on your nearest stockist of embroidery cotton, contact the following:

DMC
(also distributors of Zweigart fabrics)

UK
DMC Creative World Ltd
62 Pullman Road, Wigston
Leicester LE8 2DY
Telephone: 0116 2811040

USA
The DMC Corporation
Port Kearney Bld.
#10 South Kerney
N.J. 07032–0650
Telephone: 201 589 0606

AUSTRALIA
DMC (Australia) Pty Ltd
P.O. Box 317
Earlwood
NSW 2206
Telephone: 02 9559 3088

COATS AND ANCHOR
UK
Coats Paton Crafts
McMullen Road, Darlington
Co. Durham DL1 1YQ
Telephone: 01325 381010

USA
Coats & Clark
P.O. Box 2706 Dept COI
Greenville SC 29616
Telephone: 803 234 0103

AUSTRALIA
Coats Spencer Crafts
Level 1, 382 Wellington Rd
Mulgrave, Victoria 3170
Telephone: 03 9561 2288

MADEIRA
UK
Madeira Threads (UK) Ltd
Thirsk Industrial Park
York Road, Thirsk
North Yorkshire YO7 3BX
Telephone: 01845 524880

USA
Madeira Marketing Ltd
600 East 9th Street
Michigan City, IN 46360
Telephone: 219 873 1000

AUSTRALIA
Penguin Threads Pty Ltd
25-27 Izett Street
Prahran
Victoria 3181
Telephone: 03 9529 4400